Dear Parent:
Your child's love of readir

Every child learns to read in a different way and at his or her own speed. You can help your young reader improve and become more confident by encouraging his or her own interests and abilities. You can also guide your child's spiritual development by reading stories with biblical values and Bible stories, like I Can Read! books published by Zonderkidz. From books your child reads with you to the first books he or she reads alone, there are I Can Read! books for every stage of reading:

SHARED READING
Basic language, word repetition, and whimsical illustrations, ideal for sharing with your emergent reader.

BEGINNING READING
Short sentences, familiar words, and simple concepts for children eager to read on their own.

READING WITH HELP
Engaging stories, longer sentences, and language play for developing readers.

READING ALONE
Complex plots, challenging vocabulary, and high-interest topics for the independent reader.

ADVANCED READING
Short paragraphs, chapters, and exciting themes for the perfect bridge to chapter books.

I Can Read! books have introduced children to the joy of reading since 1957. Featuring award-winning authors and illustrators and a fabulous cast of beloved characters, I Can Read! books set the standard for beginning readers.

A lifetime of discovery begins with the magical words "I Can Read!"

Visit www.icanread.com for information on enriching your child's reading experience.
Visit www.zonderkidz.com for more Zonderkidz I Can Read! titles.

He made all kinds of creatures
that move along the ground.
And God saw that it was good.
—*Genesis 1:24-26*

ZONDERKIDZ

Spiders, Snakes, Bees, and Bats
Copyright © 2010 by Zonderkidz

Requests for information should be addressed to:
Zonderkidz, *Grand Rapids, Michigan 49530*

Library of Congress Cataloging-in-Publication Data
   Spiders, snakes, bees, and bats.
      p. cm. — (I can read!)
         ISBN 978-0-310-72007-2 (softcover)
      1. Spiders—Juvenile literature. 2. Vertebrates—Juvenile literature. I. Zonderkidz.
   QL458.4.S647 2010
   590—dc22   2009041261

Editor: Mary Hassinger
Art direction & design: Sarah Molegraaf

Printed in China

12 13 14 /DSC/ 5 4 3 2

I Can Read!

··· MADE·BY·GOD ···

Spiders, Snakes, Bees, and Bats

Contents

God made everything.

It is all good.

He made the gentle butterfly and

the hairiest, biggest…

SPIDER!

Spiders are not really insects.

They are animals called arachnids.

Spiders are found almost everywhere.

God made about 30,000 kinds

of spiders.

Most have eight legs and eight eyes.

Spiders are carnivorous.

They eat only meat.

Spiders might be pests,
but they eat many bugs that bug us,
like mosquitoes.
To help catch food, most spiders
use webs.

Spider body parts called spinnerets make silk to build webs. Webs are used as homes, to catch food, and for cocoons. There are many kinds of webs—spiral orb and funnel are two.

A well-known spider is
the tarantula.

Tarantulas are furry.

They can grow to be nine or ten

inches—like a dinner plate!

Some people have pet tarantulas.

God made everything.

It is all good.

He made the cutest puppy

and the longest, creepiest…

SNAKE!

Snakes are reptiles.

They are found almost everywhere.

Snakes live in deserts, lakes,

forests, and fields.

Snakes are covered with smooth,

dry scales that protect them.

Snakes shed their old scales.

If they do not fall off,

the snake might get sick.

Some snakes are hatched from eggs.

Others come out of their mother.

No matter how they are born,

all snakes have special bones that

twist, bend, and curl.

Snakes smell with their tongues.

The tongue collects smells.

It goes back into the snake's mouth
to a spot called Jacobson's Organ.

It tells the snake whose scent
is on the tongue.

One very tiny snake is called
a thread snake.

It eats ant and termite eggs.

The longest snakes are
pythons and anacondas.

They eat eggs, fish, frogs, and
small rodents.

If they eat a big meal, these snakes
eat only four or five times a year!

God made everything.

It is all good.

He made the prettiest rose

and the buzzing, stinging…

BEE!

Bees are insects.

They have six legs, five eyes, four
wings, a nectar pouch, and stomach.

Bees are found in many places
but do not like cold weather.

In winter, bees stay in their hive
to keep warm.

They eat the honey they made
all summer.

God made more than 10,000

kinds of bees.

Bees live in hives or nests.

A small hive may have 20,000 bees!

There is only one queen, and she is

in charge for two to three years.

The queen bee can lay
2,000 eggs every day.
She has lots of help in the hive.
Female worker bees do all the work.
There are hundreds of male bees
called drones.
The drones have no stingers.
Their main job is to help the queen
make babies.

Bees have two jobs.

Bees make honey from

pollen and nectar in flowers.

One bee visits 4,000 flowers

to make one tablespoon of honey!

When looking for pollen,

a bee can fly six miles and

travel fifteen miles an hour!

Bees have a job called pollination.

Their sticky legs help pollen

get from one plant to another.

Without the help of bees,

many plants may not grow.

God made everything.

It is all good.

He made the big, strong eagle

and the squeaky, scary-looking…

BAT!

Bats are the only flying mammal
in the world.

They use their wings for flying
and holding things like food.

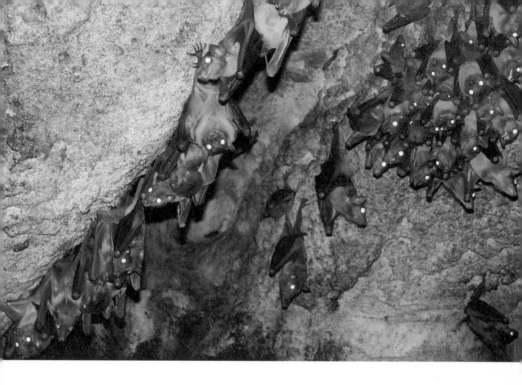

God made over 1,000 kinds of bats.

They live all over the world.

Bats sleep in roosts.

Roosts are found in places

like caves and hollow trees.

Bats sleep upside-down.

This makes it easier for them to

take off fast, if necessary.

Bats help people by eating
pesky bugs like mosquitoes.
A single brown bat can eat 1,200
mosquitoes in one hour!
Other bats eat fruit, fish, and frogs.
Bats mostly eat at night.
They use sounds that people cannot
hear to help find food in the dark.
This is called echo-location.

Bat babies are called pups.

When bats grow up, they like to live

and fly in large groups called colonies.

One of the largest colonies of bats

is in the state of Texas.

About twenty million bats

live together in one cave and share

a dinner of about 200 tons of bugs…

each night!